CAHOKIA

BY ROBERT LEROSE

Apex is distributed by North Star Editions:
sales@northstareditions.com | 888-417-0195

Produced for Apex by Red Line Editorial.

Photographs ©: Shutterstock Images, cover, 1, 4–5, 6–7, 10–11, 12–13, 15, 16–17, 18–19, 20–21, 22–23, 25, 29; National Archives and Records Administration, 8; Derik Holtmann/Belleville News Democrat/AP Images, 9; Carver Mostardi/Alamy, 13; Carol M. Highsmith/Library of Congress, 26; Sue Ogrocki/AP Images, 27

Library of Congress Control Number: 2022911842

ISBN
978-1-63738-431-2 (hardcover)
978-1-63738-458-9 (paperback)
978-1-63738-510-4 (ebook pdf)
978-1-63738-485-5 (hosted ebook)

Printed in the United States of America
Mankato, MN
012023

NOTE TO PARENTS AND EDUCATORS

Apex books are designed to build literacy skills in striving readers. Exciting, high-interest content attracts and holds readers' attention. The text is carefully leveled to allow students to achieve success quickly. Additional features, such as bolded glossary words for difficult terms, help build comprehension.

TABLE OF CONTENTS

CHAPTER 1

A CITY OF MOUNDS 4

CHAPTER 2

RISING RIVER 10

CHAPTER 3

CLEARING THE FOREST 16

CHAPTER 4

OTHER IDEAS 22

COMPREHENSION QUESTIONS • 28

GLOSSARY • 30

TO LEARN MORE • 31

ABOUT THE AUTHOR • 31

INDEX • 32

A CITY OF MOUNDS

A family stands on top of a massive mound. They can see for miles around them. The family spots many other mounds nearby. They are visiting Cahokia.

The city of Cahokia spread across more than 6 square

FAST FACT

Cahokia's tallest mound is known as Monks Mound. It is 100 feet (30 m) high.

Cahokia was once a city. People began living there in the 700s CE. They built the mounds out of dirt.

Monks Mound is one of the largest things made out of earth by people long ago.

But by 1400 CE, Cahokia was empty. Everyone had left the city. Today, archaeologists still don't know for certain what happened.

Many people visit the Cahokia mounds every year.

People help with an archaeological dig at Cahokia in 2012.

STILL STANDING

Some Cahokia mounds still stand today. They're in the state of Illinois. Archaeologists dig through the remains. They hunt for clues that might clear up the mystery.

CHAPTER 2

RISING RIVER

Cahokia ran along the banks of the Mississippi River. It was the largest urban center in the Americas. As many as 20,000 people lived in the city.

Cahokia lies across the Mississippi River from where

People started coming to Cahokia in the 700s CE. Corn was their main crop. They made pottery and carvings from copper, wood, and stone.

Corn remains a common crop in the region.

Scientists have found many pieces of pottery from digs at Cahokia.

FAST FACT

Cahokia means "wild geese" in French.

Around 1200, the Mississippi River began to rise. The land might have flooded. Crops could have failed. That might be why people left. But many scientists aren't sure flooding was the main cause.

UNKNOWN LANGUAGE

The people of Cahokia did not call their city "Cahokia." And they never wrote down their language. So, scientists don't know what the people called themselves.

The land near Cahokia continues to have floods. ▶

CHAPTER 3

CLEARING THE FOREST

Wood was a big part of life in Cahokia. The forests had lots of trees. People cut them down to build houses. They burned wood to keep warm.

Some people who traded with Cahokia were unfriendly. So, people built a large fence around the city. The tall wooden posts helped protect them.

FAST FACT

At one point, more people lived in Cahokia than in Paris, France.

The fenced-in homes in Cahokia may have looked like this.

WOODHENGE

Cahokians built circles of wooden posts. The circles were calendars. At the summer solstice, the sun rose above one post. It rose above other posts at other times of year.

Today, people call the circles of posts Woodhenge. A henge is a circle of rocks or posts.

However, making posts required cutting down more trees. Some scientists thought people left because they destroyed the forests. But most scientists disagree. They look for other reasons.

CHAPTER 4

OTHER IDEAS

Cahokia did not have a good way to get rid of garbage. As the garbage grew, many people got sick and died.

Dealing with trash remains a problem for many cities.

Scientists also think that battles took place in Cahokia. Some people would have lost their lives. Perhaps that emptied the city.

A SHORT RETURN

Cahokia was empty for many years. But new people came around 1500 CE. They farmed corn and hunted bison. Then they left the city in about 1700.

Today, people can see examples of what Cahokia's walls might have looked like.

There is some evidence that people left to join other groups. They might have wanted a better, safer life. But much about Cahokia is still a mystery.

People of the Osage Nation are connected to the people of Cahokia. Mounds are important parts of Osage culture and history.

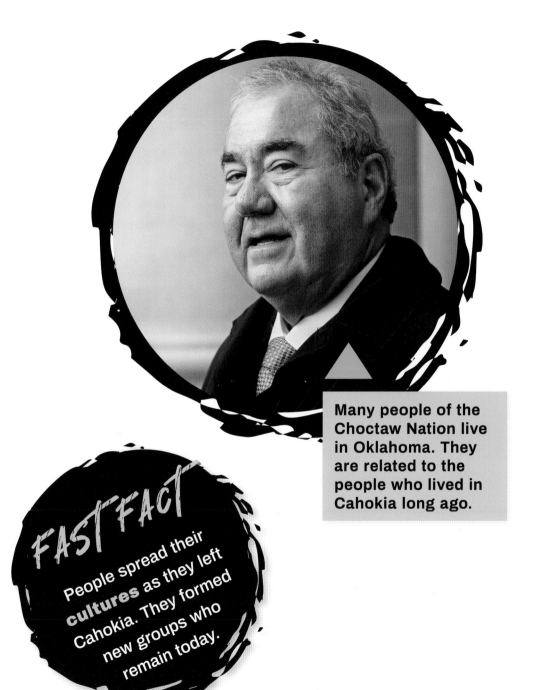

Many people of the Choctaw Nation live in Oklahoma. They are related to the people who lived in Cahokia long ago.

COMPREHENSION QUESTIONS

Write your answers on a separate piece of paper.

1. Write a sentence that explains the main idea of Chapter 3.

2. Would you have wanted to live in Cahokia? Why or why not?

3. When did the first people come to Cahokia?

> **A.** in 700 CE
> **B.** in 1200 CE
> **C.** in 1500 CE

4. Why aren't scientists sure what the people of Cahokia called themselves?

> **A.** Very few people lived in Cahokia.
> **B.** The people never wrote down their language.
> **C.** Scientists don't know where the people lived.

5. What does *protect* mean in this book?

*So, people built a large fence around the city.
The tall wooden posts helped protect them.*

    A. stop working

    B. cause danger

    C. keep safe

6. What does *remain* mean in this book?

*People spread their cultures as they left
Cahokia. They formed new groups who
remain today.*

    A. are still around

    B. no longer exist

    C. go away

Answer key on page 32.

GLOSSARY

archaeologists
People who study long-ago times, often by digging up things from the past.

cultures
Groups of people and the ways they live, including their beliefs and laws.

evidence
Information that tells what happened or if something is true.

pottery
Objects, such as bowls or vases, that are made out of clay.

remains
Things that are left behind after something is used or destroyed.

summer solstice
The day each year when one of Earth's poles is tilted closest to the sun. It is the longest day of the year.

urban
Having to do with a city.